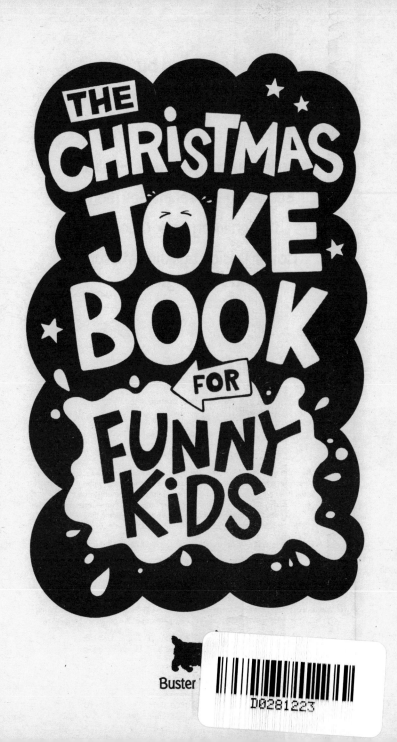

THE CHRISTMAS JOKE BOOK FOR FUNNY KIDS

Buster

Illustrated by
Andrew Pinder

Compiled by Imogen Currell-Williams

Edited by Josephine Southon

Designed by Jack Clucas

**Cover Design by Angie Allison
and John Bigwood**

First published in Great Britain in 2020 by Buster Books,
an imprint of Michael O'Mara Books Limited,
9 Lion Yard, Tremadoc Road, London SW4 7NQ

W www.mombooks.com/buster

f Buster Books

🐦 @BusterBooks

A CIP catalogue record for this book is available from the British Library.

ISBN: 978-1-78055-708-3

2 4 6 8 10 9 7 5 3 1

Papers used by Buster Books are natural, recyclable products made of wood from
well-managed, FSC®-certified forests and other controlled sources. The manufacturing
processes conform to the environmental regulations of the country of origin.

Printed and bound in October 2020 by CPI Group (UK) Ltd,
108 Beddington Lane, Croydon, CR0 4YY, United Kingdom

MIX
Paper from
responsible sources
FSC® C020471

FSC
www.fsc.org

CONTENTS

Introduction

**What happens to
naughty elves?**

They get the sack.

Welcome to this festive collection
of the best jokes for funny kids.

In this book you will find over 300 hysterical
jokes which will have you laughing your
Christmas socks off – from wintry wisecracks
and animal antics to Christmas Day crack-ups
and Santa side-splitters. If these jokes don't
tickle your funny bone over the holidays then
nothing will. Don't forget to spread the
Christmas cheer by practising your
funniest festive jokes on your
friends and family.

Santa
Side-Splitters

What's Santa's sport of choice?

North Pole-vaulting.

Why is Santa so good at karate?

Because he has a black belt.

Where does Santa go swimming?

The North Pool.

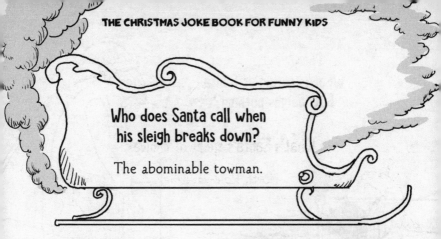

Who does Santa call when
his sleigh breaks down?

The abominable towman.

What does Santa
suffer from if he gets
stuck in a chimney?

Claus-trophobia.

How do you know
when Santa's around?

You can always
sense his presents.

What is as big as Santa but weighs nothing?

His shadow.

What's the name of Santa's measuring device?

The Santometer.

How many chimneys does Santa go down?

Stacks.

What does Santa use when he goes fishing?

His North Pole.

Where does Santa stay when he's abroad?

At a ho-ho-hotel.

What do you call Santa when he has no money?

Saint Nickel-less.

Why did Santa put his guitar in the snow?

He wanted to play some cool music.

What do you call a man who claps at Christmas?

Sant-applause.

What do you call Santa when he goes to the beach?

Sandy Claus.

What do you call Santa living at the South Pole?

A lost Claus.

Why did Santa get a parking ticket on Christmas Eve?

He left his sleigh in a snow-parking zone.

11

What goes "Ho Ho Whoosh, Ho Ho Whoosh"?

Santa stuck in
a revolving door.

Where does Santa like delivering presents?

Idaho-ho-ho.

What kind of motorbike does Santa ride?

A Holly Davidson.

What do you call Santa when he's taking a hot chocolate break?

Santa Pause.

How does Santa ask Rudolph about the weather?

"Is it going to rain, deer?"

What says "Oh oh oh"?

Santa walking backwards.

What did the sea say to Santa?

Nothing, it just waved.

Why does Santa have three gardens?

So he can hoe, hoe, hoe!

What do you get if
you cross Santa Claus
with a detective?

Santa Clues.

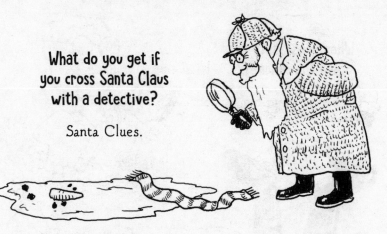

How does Santa
take photos?

With his North
Pole-aroid.

What did Santa say when he
won a saucepan in a raffle?

"That's what I call pot luck!"

When does Santa go down the chimney?

When it soots him.

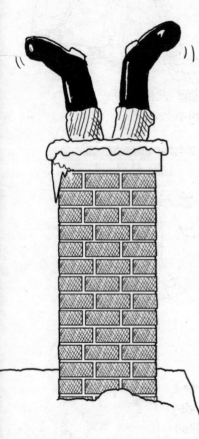

Every year, Santa delivers a present to the child of a florist ...

... He's a budding genius.

What goes red, white, red, white, red, white?

Santa rolling down a hill.

How do you know if Santa's been in your garden shed?

You've got three extra hoes.

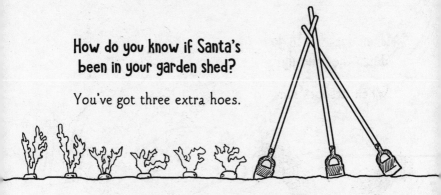

Will Santa launch an online alternative to his usual delivery service?

He's toying with the idea.

When Santa returned from his sleigh-driving test, Mrs Claus asked him if he had passed.

Santa pointed to the front of his sleigh and said, "No L plates."

Riotous
Reindeer

Why doesn't Santa use reindeer milk in his coffee?

He's on a deery-free diet.

What do you call a reindeer with three eyes?

A reiiindeer.

What game do reindeer like to play?

Stable tennis.

19

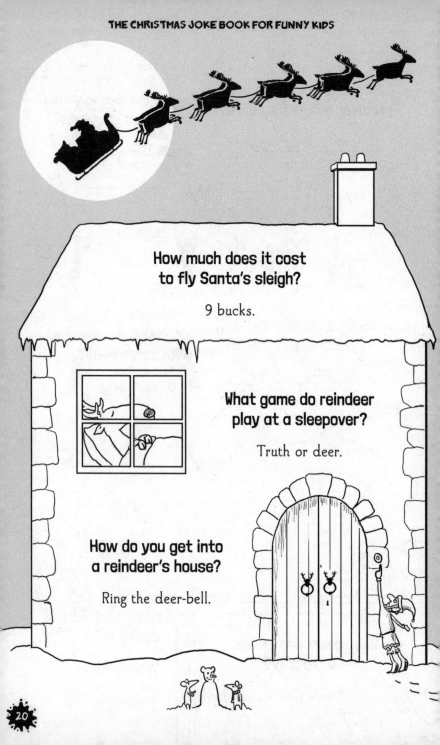

How much does it cost to fly Santa's sleigh?

9 bucks.

What game do reindeer play at a sleepover?

Truth or deer.

How do you get into a reindeer's house?

Ring the deer-bell.

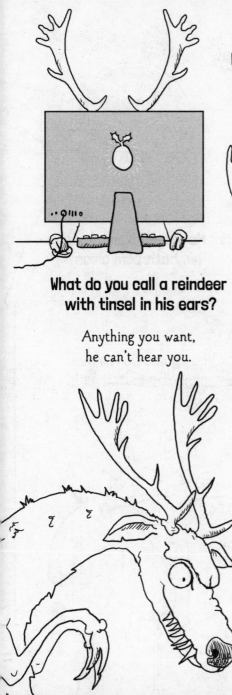

How do reindeer buy their Christmas presents?

On the antlernet.

What do you call a reindeer with tinsel in his ears?

Anything you want, he can't hear you.

What do you call a scary-looking reindeer?

A cari-boo!

Why did the reindeer put a clock on the sleigh?

Because they wanted to see time fly.

How does Santa keep his bathroom clean?

He uses Comet.

What do reindeer say before they tell a joke?

"This will sleigh you."

22

Where do Santa and his reindeer get hot chocolate when they're flying in the sky?

Star-bucks.

Why did the reindeer help the man across the road?

It would have been Rudolph him not to.

Why do reindeer like Christmas?

Because they're Santamental.

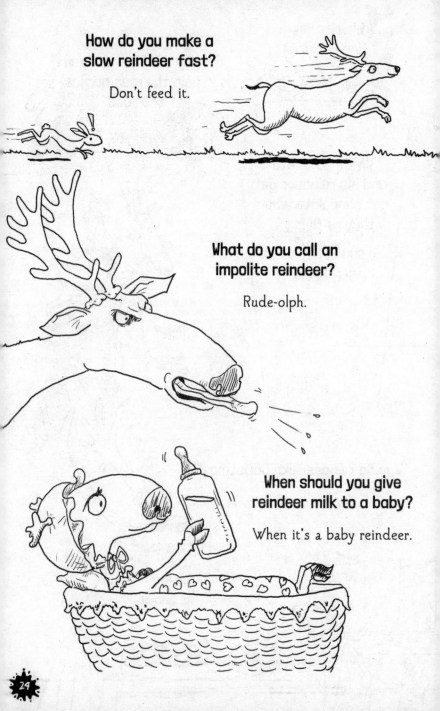

How do you make a slow reindeer fast?

Don't feed it.

What do you call an impolite reindeer?

Rude-olph.

When should you give reindeer milk to a baby?

When it's a baby reindeer.

Where do you find reindeer?

It depends where you leave them.

Why did the reindeer wear sunglasses to the Christmas party?

Because he didn't want to be recognized.

Why do reindeer wear fur coats?

Because they look silly in snowsuits.

**What's red and white and
gives presents to gazelles?**

Santelope.

**Why does Scrooge love
all of the reindeer?**

Because every buck
is dear to him.

**How does Rudolph
know when Christmas
is coming?**

He looks at
his calen-deer.

Why didn't anyone bid for Rudolph and Blitzen?

Because they were two deer.

What do you do with a blue reindeer?

Try to cheer it up.

Why did the reindeer take a ruler to bed with him?

To see how long he slept.

27

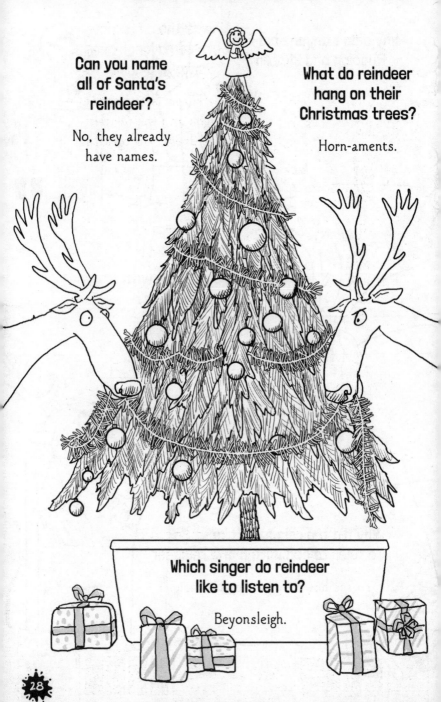

Can you name all of Santa's reindeer?

No, they already have names.

What do reindeer hang on their Christmas trees?

Horn-aments.

Which singer do reindeer like to listen to?

Beyonsleigh.

What's the difference between a knight and Santa's reindeer?

The knight is slaying the dragon and the reindeer are dragon the sleigh.

How much does it cost Santa to park his sleigh and reindeer?

Nothing, it's on the house.

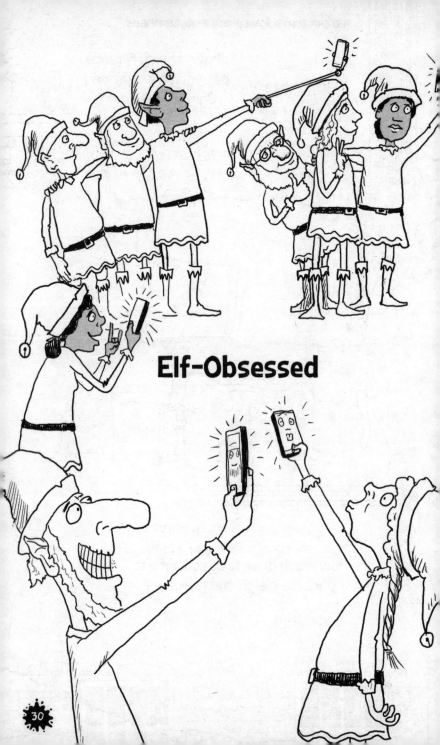

Elf-Obsessed

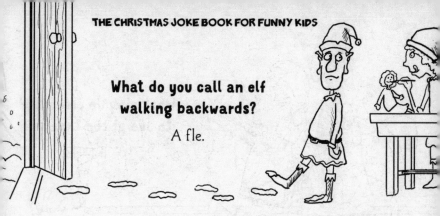

**What do you call an elf
walking backwards?**

A fle.

**How do elves
greet each other?**

"Small world, isn't it?"

**If there were eleven elves and
another one came along,
what would he be?**

The twelf.

What play do elves like to see at the theatre?

Tw-elf Night.

Did Santa's reindeer go to school?

No, they were elf-taught.

What type of photos does Santa take?

Elfies.

How did the elf build a house at the North Pole?

Iglooed it.

Why did Santa's helper want to keep the presents?

Because he was a bit elfish.

What do you call an elf who runs off and stops working for Santa?

A rebel without a Claus.

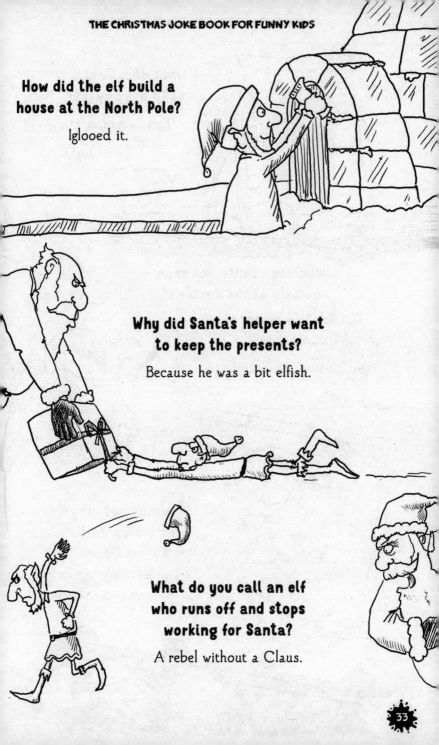

What does Santa use to bake cakes?

Elf-raising flour.

Why does Santa get seen quickly at the doctor's?

He has private elf care.

Which pop singer does Santa like to impersonate?

Elf-is Presley.

Knock Knock!

Who's there?

Elf.

Elf, who?

**Elf I knock again
will you let me in?**

**How do you
help someone
who has lost their
Christmas spirit?**

Nurse them
back to elf.

What kind of money do elves use?

Jingle bills.

Who lives at the North Pole, makes toys and rides around in a pumpkin?

Cinder-elf-a.

Why did the elves ask the turkey to join the band?

Because it had the drumsticks.

Where do elves go to dance?

Snow balls.

Why did the elf put his bed in a fireplace?

He wanted to sleep like a log.

How many elves does it take to change a light bulb?

Ten. One to change the bulb, and nine to stand on each other's shoulders.

What do elves eat for breakfast?

Ice Crispies.

What do you call a frozen elf hanging from the ceiling?

An elficle.

What do elves cook with in the kitchen?

Utinsels.

**What do you call an elf
who won the lottery?**

Welfy.

**What cars do
elves drive?**

Toyotas.

**Why did Santa's helper
see the doctor?**

Because he had
low elf-esteem.

How long are an elf's legs?

Just long enough to reach the ground.

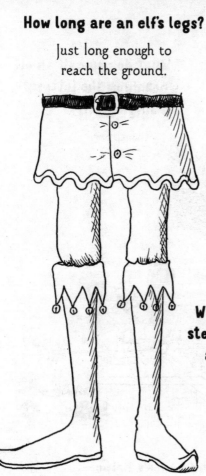

What do you call an elf who steals gift wrap from the rich and gives it to the poor?

Ribbon Hood.

What happens to naughty elves?

They get the sack.

What do you call a singing elf?

A wrapper.

What do elves do after school?

Their gnomework.

If an athlete gets athlete's foot, what does an elf get?

Mistle toe.

41

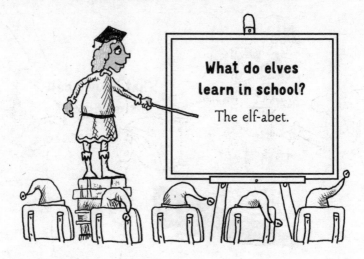

What do elves learn in school?

The elf-abet.

What kind of bread do elves make sandwiches with?

Shortbread.

What did the elf say will be the first step in using a computer?

"First, yule log on."

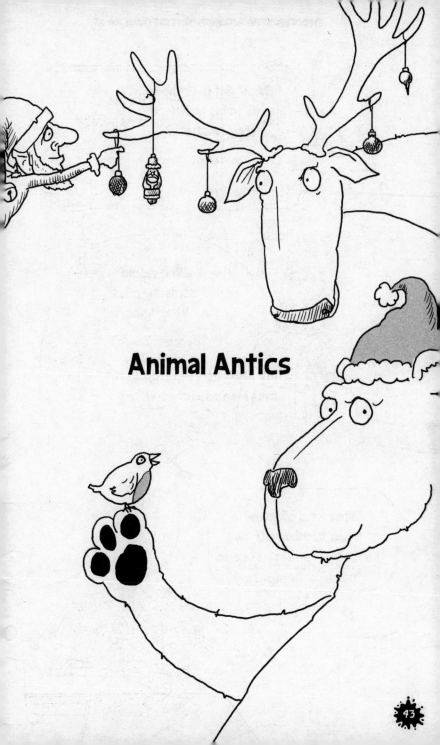

Animal Antics

What did the rabbit give to his girlfriend for Christmas?

A 24-carrot ring.

Why would someone miss their igloo?

Because there's snow place like home.

What kind of jokes do turtles tell?

Shell-arious ones.

What's twenty metres tall, has sharp teeth and goes "Ho, ho, ho"?

Tyranno-santa rex.

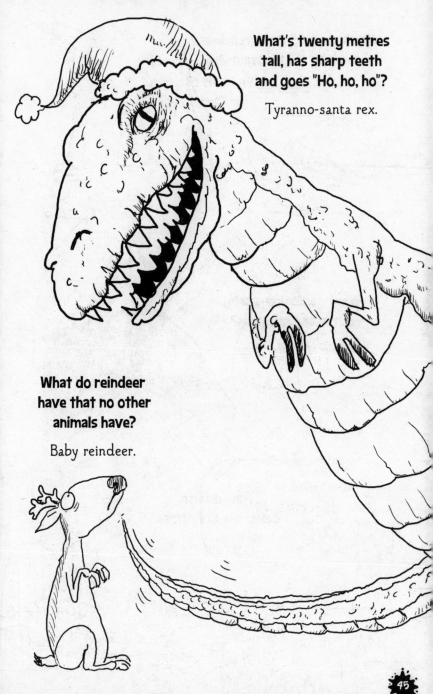

What do reindeer have that no other animals have?

Baby reindeer.

Which one of Santa's reindeer terrifies the dinosaurs?

Comet.

What do donkeys send out near Christmas?

Mule-tide greetings.

How do fish celebrate Christmas?

They hang reefs on the door.

Which birds are good at writing Christmas cards?

Pen-guins.

Why don't mussels give presents at Christmas?

Because they're shell-fish.

What do you call a cat in the desert at Christmas?

Sandy Claws.

Why wouldn't the cat climb the Christmas tree at night?

It was afraid of the bark.

What did the beaver say to the Christmas tree?

"Nice gnawing you."

**Who delivers presents
to baby sharks at
Christmas?**

Santa Jaws.

**What's green, covered in
tinsel and goes "croak"?**

A mistle-toad.

Knock Knock!

Who's there?

Rabbit.

Rabbit, who?

**Rabbit up carefully please,
this present is fragile.**

Knock Knock!

Who's there?

Icy.

Icy, who?

Icy a big polar bear up ahead.

Which one of Santa's reindeer has the best moves?

Dancer.

What's white, lives at the North Pole and runs around without any clothes on?

A polar bare.

What do you get when you cross a bell with a skunk?

Jingle smells.

Why don't penguins fly?

Because they're not tall enough to be pilots.

What do sheep say to each other at Christmas?

"Merry Christmas to ewe!"

What do fish sing at Christmastime?

Christmas corals.

What do angry mice send to each other in December?

Cross-mouse cards.

What do wild animals sing at Christmas?

Jungle bells, jungle bells, jungle all the way.

Which Christmas carol do dogs like to sing?

Bark the Herald Angels Sing.

What did the reindeer say to the elf?

Nothing ... Reindeer can't talk.

Why did the turkey cross the road?

He wasn't a chicken.

What do you call a one-eyed deer who lends a helping hand?

A good eye-deer.

Who delivers your dog's Christmas presents?

Santa Paws.

**How do you know
if Santa is really
a werewolf?**

He has Santa Claws.

Knock Knock!

Who's there?

Centipede.

Centipede, who?

**Centipede on the
Christmas tree!**

Food Festivities

Can a chicken jump higher than the Empire State Building?

Yes, of course - a building can't jump at all.

What do you call a train loaded with Christmas toffees?

A chew chew train.

Why is everyone so thirsty at the North Pole?

There's no well, no well.

57

What does Santa eat for breakfast?

Mistle-toast.

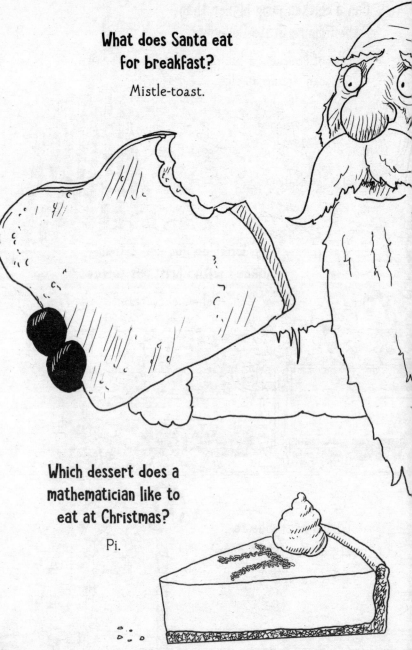

Which dessert does a mathematician like to eat at Christmas?

Pi.

Doctor: What seems to be the problem?

Santa: I have a pie stuck to my bottom.

Doctor: You're in luck. I have some cream for that.

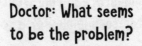

Dad: We're having grandma for Christmas dinner.

Me: Really? I thought we were having ham.

A gingerbread man went to the doctor complaining of a sore knee.

"A sore knee?" the doctor asked. "Have you tried icing it?"

Knock Knock!

Who's there?

Arthur.

Arthur, who?

Arthur any roast potatoes left?

Knock Knock!

Who's there?

Lettuce.

Lettuce, who?

Lettuce in for cocoa and Christmas cookies.

What do vampires put on their Christmas dinner?

Grave-y.

Why is the ocean full of currents this year?

Because last year's fruitcake was so awful I threw it in the ocean.

"This Christmas dinner is disgusting!"

"Well, you asked for a fowl roast."

Why did the children start eating the puzzle on Christmas day?

Because their uncle said it was a piece of cake.

Why did the gingerbread man go to the doctor?

Because he was feeling crummy.

Why is the turkey such a fashionable bird?

Because he's always well-dressed when he comes to dinner.

Why should Christmas dinner always be well done?

So you can say "Merry Crispness".

What's the best thing to put into Christmas dinner?

Your teeth.

What does Santa put on his toast?

Jingle jam.

Who was the most famous carolling herb?

Elvis Parsley.

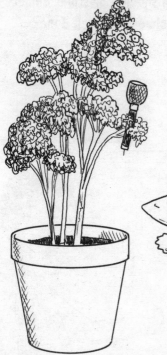

What do crackers and nuts remind me of?

You.

Where would you find chilli beans?

At the North Pole.

What's the most popular Christmas wine?

"But I don't like Brussels sprouts."

How do cranberries greet each other during the holidays?

"Berry Christmas!"

What did the gingerbread man put on his bed?

A baking sheet.

What happens if you eat too many Christmas decorations?

You get tinsel-itis.

Who hides in a bakery at Christmas?

An apple spy.

Who beats his chest and swings from Christmas cake to Christmas cake?

Tarzipan.

Knock Knock!

Who's there?

Canoe.

Canoe, who?

Canoe help me bake some Christmas cookies?

Why doesn't Santa eat junk food?

Because it's bad for your elf.

What kind of cakes do snowmen like?

The kind with lots of frosting.

Christmas Day Crack-Ups

What did the bald man say when he got a comb for Christmas?

"Thanks, I'll never part with it."

Why did Scrooge buy everyone birds for Christmas?

Because they were going cheep.

Knock Knock!

Who's there?

Chris.

Chris, who?

Christmas is here!

Why did the Christmas tree go to the barber?

It needed to be trimmed.

What did one Christmas tree say to the other?

"We have great chemis-tree."

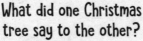

The only Christmas present I got this year was a pack of playing cards ...

... I find that very hard to deal with.

My Christmas cardigan
keeps giving me
electric shocks ...

... I took it back
and exchanged it for
another one. It was
free of charge.

I got a universal remote
control for Christmas ...

... This changes everything.

I have this incredible ability
to predict what's inside
a wrapped present.

It's a gift.

Where do you keep a Christmas tree?

Between a Christmas two and a Christmas four.

How do Christmas angels greet each other?

"Halo."

Why do mummies like Christmas so much?

Because of all the wrapping.

What did one Christmas
light say to the other?

"You light
me up."

Why didn't the rope get
any Christmas presents?

It had been knotty.

What do you call cutting
down a Christmas tree?

Christmas chopping.

Why are Christmas trees so fond of the past?

Because the present's beneath them.

Why did Scrooge keep a pet lamb?

Because it would say "Baaaaahh humbug".

Which king do children like to visit at Christmas?

A stoc-king.

What part of the body do you only see at Christmas?

Mistle-toe.

Why is it getting harder to buy advent calendars?

Because their days are numbered.

How did Scrooge win the basketball game?

The ghost of Christmas passed.

What's the best Christmas present in the world?

A broken drum.
You just can't beat it.

What's the best thing to give your parents for Christmas?

A list of everything you want.

What happened to the man who stole an advent calendar?

He got 25 days.

Knock Knock!

Who's there?

Mary.

Mary, who?

Mary Christmas.

What do you call a Christmas tree with a big nose?

Pine-occhio.

Why are Christmas trees bad knitters?

They keep dropping their needles.

What did one Christmas tree decoration say to the other?

"Let's hang out."

Where did the mistletoe
go to become famous?

Holly-wood.

What's the difference between
the Christmas alphabet and
the normal alphabet?

The Christmas
alphabet has no 'L'.

Why didn't the skeleton go
to the Christmas party?

He had no body to go with.

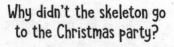

What comes at the end of Christmas day?

The letter 'Y'.

What did the fireman's wife get for Christmas?

A ladder in her stocking.

What did the stamp say to the Christmas card?

"Stick with me and we'll go places."

Snowman
Shenanigans

What do snowmen like to do at the weekend?

Chill out.

What do snowmen eat for lunch?

Icebergers.

Where do snowmen keep their money?

In a snowbank.

What classroom exercise do they do at snowman school?

Snow and tell.

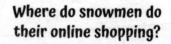

Where do snowmen do their online shopping?

On the winternet.

What's worse than a reindeer with a runny nose?

A snowman with a fever.

What did the snowman say to the annoying carrot?

"Get out of my face."

How do you scare a snowman?

With a hairdryer.

How does one snowman greet another?

"Ice to meet you."

What do snowmen call their offspring?

Chill-dren.

What do you call a snowman party?

A snowball.

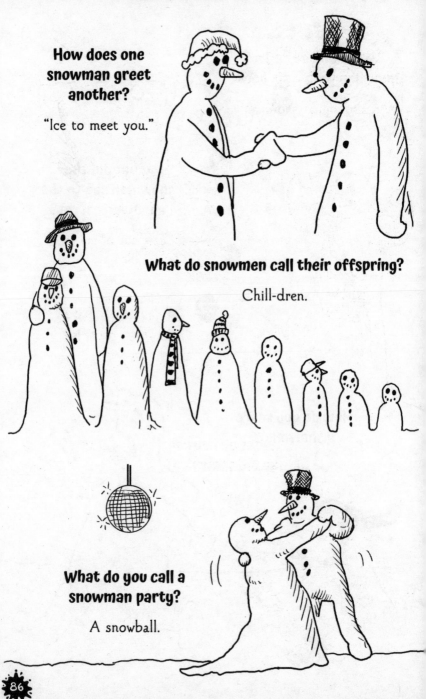

What do you call a snowman with a six pack?

An abdominal snowman.

What do you call a snowman on skis?

A snowmobile.

What do you call an old snowman?

A puddle.

What did the policeman say when he saw a snowman stealing carrots?

"Freeze."

What do you get when you cross a snowman and a baker?

Frosty the Dough-man.

What are a snowman's favourite letters?

I. C.

What does a snowman drink to stay warm?

Iced tea.

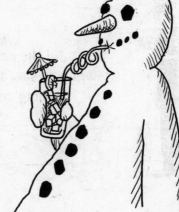

Which family member do snowmen visit at Christmas?

Aunt Arctica.

What do snowmen like to put on their lunch?

Chilly sauce.

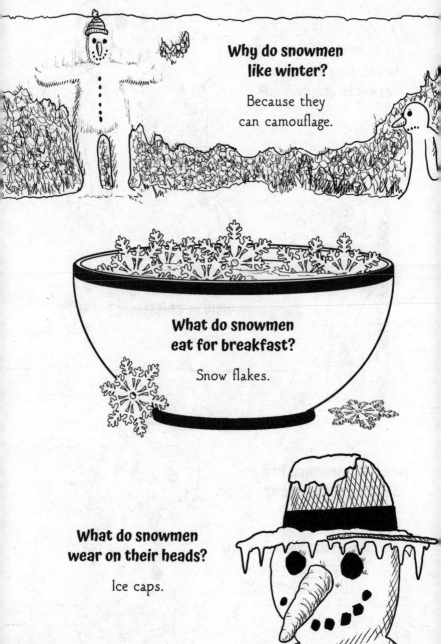

Why do snowmen like winter?

Because they can camouflage.

What do snowmen eat for breakfast?

Snow flakes.

What do snowmen wear on their heads?

Ice caps.

Why do snowmen like living at the North Pole?

Because it's cool.

What do they sing at a snowman's birthday party?

"Freeze a jolly good fellow."

Why was the snowman rummaging in the bag of carrots?

He was picking his nose.

What did the snowman say when the robin asked for directions?

"I have snow idea."

What do you get when you cross a snowman with a vampire?

Frostbite.

What did one snowman say to the other?

"Can you smell carrots?"

Why don't snowmen like carrot cake?

Because it tastes like bogies.

What do you call a snowman's dog?

A slush puppy.

Why is it dangerous for a snowman to be angry?

It might have a meltdown.

How do snowmen get around?

By icicle.

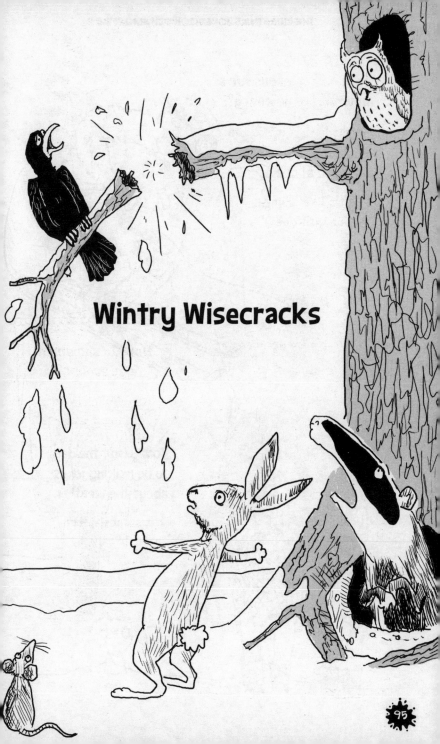

Wintry Wisecracks

Cyclopes are really good at skiing.

It's like skiing, but with one 'i'.

Today isn't the day to be making jokes about the weather.

It's snow joke.

What did the snowflake say to the fallen leaf?

You are so last season.

What subject do snowy owls like to study?

Owl-gebra.

What sits at the bottom of the Arctic Ocean and shakes?

A nervous wreck.

What can you catch in the winter with your eyes closed?

A cold.

If the sun shines while it's snowing, what should you look for?

Snowbows.

Knock Knock!

Who's there?

Snow.

Snow, who?

Snow one's at the door.

What do you call a slow skier?

A slopepoke.

What sort of ball doesn't bounce?

A snow ball.

What falls but never hurts itself?

Snow.

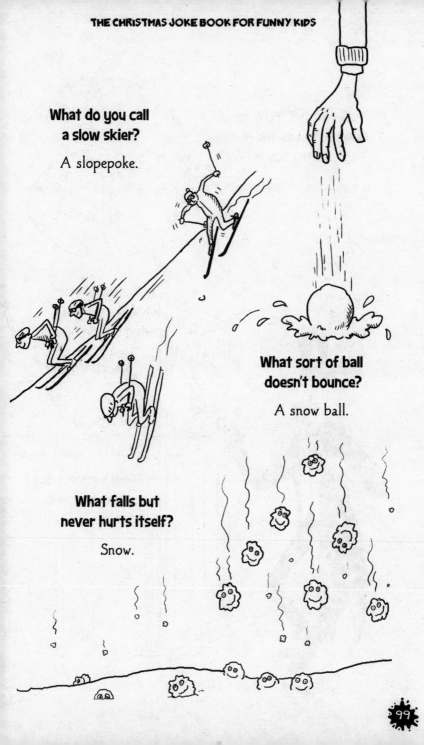

How much difference is there between the North Pole and the South Pole?

All the difference in the world.

Knock Knock!

Who's there?

Snow.

Snow, who?

Snow business like show business.

Why is it difficult to keep a secret in the North Pole?

Because your teeth chatter.

What's the most competitive season?

Win-ter.

How do you lift a frozen car?

With a Jack Frost.

I got hit in the face with a snowball recently ...

... Knocked me out cold.

What do you get when you cross a pine cone and a polar bear?

A fur tree.

Why is it so cold at Christmas?

Because it's in Decembrrrrrr.

102

Knock Knock!

Who's there?

Emma.

Emma, who?

Emma bit cold out here ... Let me in!

Why do bees stay in the hive in winter?

Swarm.

What does a cyclist ride in the winter?

An icicle.

How do you stop your feet getting cold?

Don't walk around brrr-footed.

What did the hat say to the scarf?

"You hang around while I go on ahead."

When are your eyes not eyes?

When the cold winter wind makes them water.

Knock Knock!

Who's there?

Howard.

Howard, who?

Howard you like to stand out in the cold while someone keeps asking "Who's there?"

**How does Good
King Wenceslas
like his pizzas?**

Deep pan,
crisp and even.

**When is a boat like
a heap of snow?**

When it comes
a-drift.

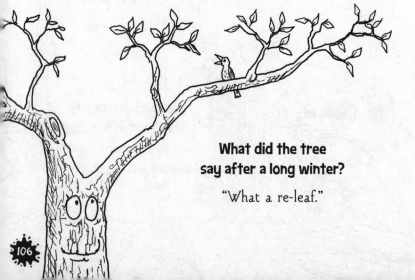

**What did the tree
say after a long winter?**

"What a re-leaf."

Chucklesome Tunes

Which famous singer do Christmas trees listen to?

Spruce Springsteen.

Knock Knock!

Who's there?

Olive.

Olive, who?

Olive the other reindeer used to laugh and call him names ...

Knock Knock!

Who's there?

Oh, Chris.

Oh, Chris, who?

**Oh, Christmas tree,
Oh, Christmas tree ...**

**Why was the Christmas
caroller locked out?**

He couldn't find his key.

Knock Knock!

Who's there?

Oakham.

Oakham, who?

**Oakham all
ye faithful ...**

**Why didn't Rudolph
get a good report?**

Because he went
down in History.

**What do hip-hop artists
do on Christmas day?**

Unwrap.

**Why did the choir have to
cancel their carol concert?**

They caught tinsel-itis.

Knock Knock!

Who's there?

Honda.

Honda, who?

**Honda first day
of Christmas,
my true love
sent to me ...**

What kind of key
do you need for
a nativity play?

A don-key.

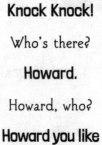

Knock Knock!

Who's there?

Howard.

Howard, who?

**Howard you like
to sing Christmas
carols with me?**

Where do you find the most singers on Christmas Eve?

North Carol-ina.

What Christmas carol is sung in the desert?

O Camel, Ye Faithful.

Why were the carollers arrested?

They were in big treble.

What does Santa say when he has a hard decision to make?

"I'm between a jingle bell rock and a hard place."

Knock Knock!

Who's there?

Harold.

Harold, who?

Harold angels sing.

What do you give to Christmas carollers?

Some har-money.

What is a parent's preferred
Christmas carol?

Silent Night.

Knock Knock!

Who's there?

Wayne.

Wayne, who?

Wayne in a manger.

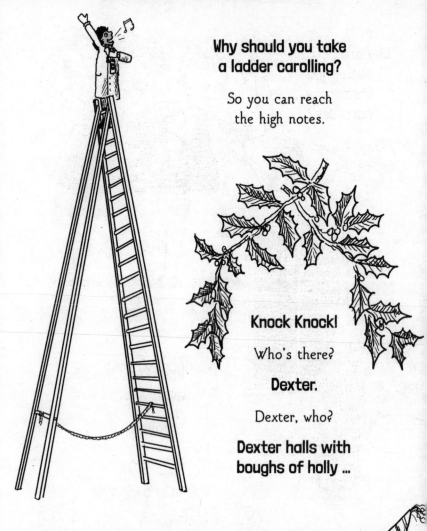

Why should you take a ladder carolling?

So you can reach the high notes.

Knock Knock!

Who's there?

Dexter.

Dexter, who?

Dexter halls with boughs of holly ...

Who gets invited to the most holiday parties?

Christmas Carol.

116

Why are pirates such good Christmas carollers?

They're used to hitting the high C.

Knock Knock!

Who's there?

Ima.

Ima, who?

Ima dreaming of a white Christmas ...

What do you call a bunch of chess players showing off in a hotel lobby?

Chess nuts boasting in an open foyer.

Knee-Slapping Knock Knocks

Knock Knock!

Who's there?

Avery.

Avery, who?

**Avery Merry
Christmas to you!**

Knock Knock!

Who's there?

Coal.

Coal, who?

**Coal me when
Santa's on his way.**

Knock Knock!

Who's there?

Gladys.

Gladys, who?

**Gladys Christmas,
aren't you?**

Knock Knock!

Who's there?

Yah.

Yah, who?

**Wow, you're really excited
about Christmas!**

Knock Knock!

Who's there?

Santa.

Santa, who?

**Santa Christmas
card to you.
Did you get it?**

Knock Knock!

Who's there?

Interrupting Santa.

Inter-

**Ho ho ho! Merry
Christmas!**

Knock Knock!

Who's there?

Pikachu.

Pikachu, who?

Pikachu Christmas presents and you'll be in trouble.

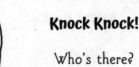

Knock Knock!

Who's there?

Harry.

Harry, who?

Harry up and open your gift!

Knock Knock!

Who's there?

Norway.

Norway, who?

Norway am I kissing anyone under the mistletoe!

Knock Knock!

Who's there?

Anita.

Anita, who?

Anita ride, Rudolph.

Knock Knock!

Who's there?

Alaska.

Alaska, who?

**Alaska again.
What do you want
for Christmas?**

Knock Knock!

Who's there?

Kanye.

Kanye, who?

**Kanye help me
untangle my
Christmas lights?**

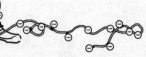

Knock Knock!

Who's there?

Tank.

Tank, who?

Tank you for my Christmas present!

Knock Knock!

Who's there?

Mary and Abby.

Mary and Abby, who?

Mary Christmas and Abby New Year!

Knock Knock!

Who's there?

Irish.

Irish, who?

**Irish you a
Merry Christmas!**

Knock Knock!

Who's there?

Ivana.

Ivana, who?

**Ivana wish you a
Merry Christmas.**

Knock Knock!

Who's there?

Wooden shoe.

Wooden shoe, who?

**Wooden shoe
you like to know
what I got you
for Christmas!**

Knock Knock!

Who's there?

Holly.

Holly, who?

**Holly-days are
here again.**